The Valley Girl Turns 40

✦

Laura Ross

iUniverse, Inc.
New York   Bloomington

The Valley Girl Turns 40

iUniverse books may be ordered through booksellers or by contacting:

iUniverse
1663 Liberty Drive
Bloomington, IN 47403
www.iuniverse.com
1-800-Authors (1-800-288-4677)

Because of the dynamic nature of the Internet, any Web addresses or links contained in this book may have changed since publication and may no longer be valid. The views expressed in this work are solely those of the author and do not necessarily reflect the views of the publisher, and the publisher hereby disclaims any responsibility for them.

ISBN: 978-0-595-52933-9 (pbk)
ISBN: 978-0-595-62984-8 (ebk)

Printed in the United States of America

Dedication

I dedicate this book to my husband, Mark, for always believing in me and all my crazy ideas. You are so mondo cool, babe!

Acknowledgments

I want to thank my children, Matt and Kayla, who definitely had to hear way more about the eighties than they ever wanted too. You guys are super awesome! I love you!

To my wonderful parents, even though, Dad, you aren't here with us anymore. I want to thank you and Mom for putting up with me in the eighties, through my teenage years. I never went a day without feeling loved by you both!

To my brothers and sisters, Adam, Danny, Julie, Kelli, and Robbie, when it comes to siblings you guys are totally stellar. I loved growing up with my very own Brady Bunch, and yes, grandma is Alice. McDonald Bunch, you are the best! XOXO!

Last but certainly not least, my chick clique Anna, Rynette, Carolyn, Janet, and Gina! I love the eighties because of you! You guys are so way beyond fantabulous, and I am one super lucky chick to have a posse like you! Thanks for all the fun and memories.

Contents

Like, Whatever

Totally Bogus

It's like so totally bogus, you know? Like, one minute we're sixteen and we are so totally cute and we are like, shopping and hanging out, cruising in the convertible Caddy, listening to the Go-Go's, and then, wham (not the band, although they were so bitchen!) But like wham! We are FORTY YEARS OLD! The Caddy is now a minivan. We shop for groceries, not clothes. We drive to do errands and chauffeur kids, not cruise and hang out, and we are definitely, most definitely, not as cute. What happened to us? Where has the time gone? I want to go back! I miss the hair, the music, the clothes. I miss the eighties. I miss being a Valley Girl. She was the eighties. She was who we were. She is why we are who we are today. Like, I am so totally sure!

Looking back is such a trip for me. I loved being a teenager and I loved being a Valley Girl. I wish I knew then what I know now. But I am sure this won't be the only time in my life I am going to say that.

My thirteen-year-old daughter is amused at the lingo of the Valley Girl. Although some of the verbiage has carried on into the, "like," next generation. Man, that word "like" is so totally— there's another one that's hard to get out of your vocabulary. It takes discipline, fer sure.

High School, youth, Valley Girls, the eighties. Wow, what bitchen times. The music, ah, it still makes me dance. The style, the hair, the cars, the movies, the guys— they were all so totally awesome. Our youth was like mondo cool, you know. It was a tubular time in America to be a teenager. Sure, we had our share of all the teen problems: peer pressure, drugs, sex, alcohol, super gnarly girlfriend bitch battles. But there was never anything we couldn't get through with the help of Madonna on the radio, a clove cigarette, or a shopping mall. Times were so different back then. It was so truly bitchen.

I mean, sure, you can expect clothes and hairstyles to change from decade to decade, but so many things have changed since the eighties. It is like some of the things we had, used or wanted, have even become antiques. Barf me out, I am so sure. I can't believe in today's world, Van Halen is considered classic rock and kids today think that Def Leppard has something to do with a hearing impaired animal! Truthfully, it really hit me when I was watching a new TV show and Molly Ringwald was playing the mother of two teenage girls. Ouch! I actually think my wrinkles were hurting at that point! I mean, when we were sixteen, we certainly had our things that defined us as Valley Girls. I guess I need to just get used to the things of today that define us as forty-year-old Valley Girls.

Trading in at Forty, Then and Now

Then/ Now

- Walkman/iPod
- wine cooler/Starbucks
- typewriter/keyboard
- thongs/flip flops
- undies/thongs
- cigarettes/Altoids
- Reebok high tops/Jimmy Choos
- Sun-In-Spray/ 100% Grey Coverage
- big bangs/ swept bangs
- curling iron/ ceramic flat iron
- Levis 501s/Levis Low Rise Flare
- flats/wedges
- totally awesome tan/white wrinkles
- collars up/collars down
- gold /silver
- eyeliner inside the eyelid/eyeliner outside the eyelid (thank God)

- Ford Mustang/Ford Minivan
- unicorns/golden retrievers
- jumpsuits/Juicy Couture sweat suits
- fast food/salad
- Slurpees/Diet Coke
- perms/highlights
- wall phone with 20-foot cord/cell phone
- shoulder pads/spaghetti strap

So like, it's not all bad. I mean, I'm so totally happy, I'm not a forty-year-old still wearing a one-piece jumpsuit with shoulder pads, my collar up, in white Reebok high tops, with Sun-In'-ed, spiral permed hair, holding a wine cooler in one hand and a Walkman in the other. Like, totally barf me out. It looked great on me in the eighties at sixteen, but there comes a time when enough is enough! I'm liking my ceramic flat ironed, 100 percent gray-covered hair, which goes with my super cute Juicy sweat suit (collar down), Starbucks in one hand, iPod in the other. Like, it totally works for me now.

Fashionista Divas

Hair

Hair has changed a lot from our big-hair Valley Girl days. Oh, and what awesome days they were! The eighties had its own distinctive, most awesome look. Whether it was crimped, feathered, straight, spiral permed, bobbed, or asymmetrical, we Vals wore it to perfection. It was an art—especially the bangs. I mean, Aqua Net should have given an award to the girl who had the biggest, most vicious bangs! It took great skill and much time to create the look. I had bangs so big and so perfect guys used to tell me they could hang ten off the top of my head. They were the perfect wave.

Then in the nineties, when we had to grow those things out (which I'm hoping most of you did grow them out), took an amazing amount of skill and technique as well. So, I say cheers to us all who worked it, wore it, and grew it!

THE MULLET

You should totally just do a Google search. Type in "the mullet" and you will laugh your heart out. The scariest thing about the mullet is it wasn't just a guy's do; it was actually worn by girls too. Grody to the max! Definitely not Valley Girls. The haircut lived out its popularity between the late seventies all the way through the early nineties, which means we Vals had to look at it all through the eighties. Much too long, like totally barf me out fer sure.

THE HAIR BEAR

Okay, you know, I loved the big hair of the eighties, but there was this other big hairstyle we Vals liked to call the "hair bears." Remember the hair bears? Oh my gosh! This style was so way out of control. The girls who wore it had to seriously maneuver their way through a doorway. It was obscenely big and much too perfect. It resembled an old lady roller set on top, and then the rest looked like they turned on a fan and hair sprayed it out so it was literally standing on end. It was such a trippy do.

Banana clip

Oh like, come on, you know you had your moment in time when you were addicted to this clip. It was a long plastic comb that closed itself along the entire back of your head. You could say it gave the effect of a horse's mane. Not to mention the thing gave you a horse-sized headache after a day's wear. This was one hair fashion I was glad to say, *good-bye to you.*

THE TAIL

I never understood the tail. Why would anyone want to walk around with their hair short all over and then have this long, scrawny-looking, ragged out hair in the middle of their neck that actually resembled a rat's tail? It was total puke city. Gag me with some Decon fer sure!

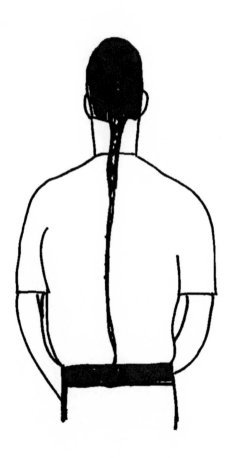

Punk

I loved eighties punk rockers. They were so edgy. Their Mohawks and spiked hair were always hot pink or black. There were no rules to it, just shave, spike, and funk your hair any way and it was cool. It was just a fun time to be a punker.

NEW WAVE

When you think of eighties new wave hair, who else but the Flock of Seagulls comes to mind? This was truly a tripindicular hair-do. It was cut and formed in many variations, but it was definitely worn best by their lead singer, Mike Score. But I, like, totally have to say, personally, if a hair stylist in the eighties suggested it for me, *I would have run, run so far away.*

THE CRIMPED LOOK

I liked the crimper. It gave us a cool kind of Tina Turner look. It was a little puffy, but it was an eighties look that was fun and easy to achieve. I just remember how hot that crimping iron got. I left it on one day on my carpet in my room and it burned a hole right through the middle of my floor! Oh well, at least my hair looked cute.

THE SIDE PONYTAIL

Funny thing is, some of you are still wearing it. Wow ladies, you're not fourteen anymore. You might want to stop being such a total Joanie and move the pony to the back of your head. I wonder if all those years of wearing the side pony has done brain damage? Maybe that would explain why you still wear it.

THE ROCKER

The heavy metal rockers of the eighties, like, kind of wore all styles combined into one. It was a spiky, spiraled permed, bi-level mullet, with the bigness of the hair bear. Then to top off this gnarly do, most of the hair came to a longer point in the back that once again resembled that ragged- out tail look. It was worn by most of our favorite rockers and many eighties dudes. Oh, and what a *motley crue* they were.

Bi-level

All right I admit it. I had a bi-level haircut. But only one, and I grew it out as fast as I could. It was towards the late eighties when it was cut in a sharp angle across the ear, leaving a fringe that swept like soft sideburns. I know what you're thinking, but like I said, I grew it out right away. It was total puke city.

HAIR AT FORTY

Being a hairdresser, I can tell you first hand that hair at forty is way different than hair at sixteen. Most of us by now have experienced at least one gray hair. Ha! Who am I kidding? Most of us by now are searching for 200 percent gray coverage, because the 100 percent isn't covering enough. Well, I can assure you at least this: hair products are so much better now than they were in the eighties. Wow, did I just say that? It's hard to believe, but yes, it's true. There are some really great styling and coloring products out there. Here is my professional opinion of must-haves at forty.

HAIR COLOR

You *must* use a professional hair color line. Stop doing your roots out of a box. If budget is a problem, then at least go into a beauty supply and get a professional line.

HAIR PRODUCTS.

It's real simple: if you only paid ninety-nine cents for your shampoo and conditioner, you shouldn't even wash your car with it. It's totally bogus stuff. You really should consider cutting out a couple lattes a month and invest in some tubular hair-care products. You don't have to spend a fortune. There are many lines that offer quality without the bankruptcy price tag.

So I say, embrace your gnarly gray hair by coloring it a beautiful shade of blonde, brown, or red! Get yourself some killer shampoo, conditioner, and styling products. After all, younger, healthy hair will make you feel young and don't we all want to be *forever young?*

Makeup

Whoa! What the heck were we thinking? Make up in the eighties was truly scruff. I mean, what's with the colors? I think the makeup colors must have been dyed with Jelly Bellies (it probably had something to do with Ronald Reagan). I'm so sure, eye shadows and lipsticks were so bright and bold—even neon. Pink, blue, and teal ruled the color palettes, unless you were goth or punk, then you had lots of black eyeliner on with your bright pink, blue, and teal. Like seriously, barf me out! Where was M.A.C when we needed them? The sad thing for us Vals is that at the one time in our lives when we really didn't need a lot of makeup, we wore it like whores. It was the eighties, for heaven's sake. It was big hair and big makeup!

Oh well, it's not all bad. We can look back and chuckle. It was the only time in our lives we'd ever consider wearing neon green mascara and peachy salmon lipstick together. Gag me with an eyelash curler, fer sure!

One of my fondest makeup faux pas was a certain lipstick called Mauve on White, by Wet n Wild. C'mon, you know you wore it. It was kind of a dead grayish pink color with a chalky white sheen to it. MMMM, pretty. Gag-o-rama, totally. But my chick clique and I wore it with pride and confidence.

Like I said, makeup was heavy in the eighties: heavy on the eyes and even heavier on the cheeks. Nothing says Valley Girl like tons of blue eyeliner rimming the inside of your eyes. We loved our roll-on lip gloss, and don't forget the Lee Press-On Nails. Makeup was even worn by guys back then. Duran Duran, Twisted Sister, Boy George— even Billy Idol had his hay day with the black eyeliners of the eighties. It was truly the era of cosmetics.

I know we all like to be *pretty in pink,* but at forty, make up should be done in more neutral tones. Everyone's eyes, lips, and face are shaped so differently. One way of wearing eye shadows and mascara doesn't work for everyone. Remember Tammy Faye Bakker? As if I need to say anything more!

At forty, we have also realized that make-up is only as great as the skin under it. Unfortunately, we were the "fake and bake" generation. If we weren't lying out completely covered in oil, literally sizzling in the California sun, we were inside our own micro-rotisseries baking ourselves in a tanning bed. Sure we were temporarily tanned, but now we are left with tons of white wrinkles that are lacking in moisture. It's okay, we just have to realize *every rose has its thorns* and make the best out of the damage we have caused. I have three words for you: exfoliate, moisturize, and SPF.

There are many great exfoliators on the market, and once you get that dead layer off you need a good moisturizer to replenish. Oh, and don't forget to slather on the sunscreen—a word that didn't exist in a Valley Girl's vocabulary until it was too late. So totally bogus, I know.

Clothes

The clothes in the eighties were so much fun with a few minor exceptions, like neon. There we go again with the neon. Who decided on this stuff? Neon is never good unless you work in construction or something. It made everyone who wore it look diseased. Secondly, I have to say, spandex was a poor fashion choice in the eighties. Even if you were the cutest Val and you had the most vicious bod, you still had a lump or bump or two. It was just weird to wear hot pink leopard spandex pants. Not a great look, but those are the exceptions. The rest was soooo bitchen. There has never been anything like it. One of my favorite fashions of the eighties was the Madonna look. I definitely had my phase of blonde scrunched hair with black lace ribbon tied in it, black Ray Ban shades, a ripped jean jacket, ripped lace gloves, and black penny loafers with white ankle socks. Oh, and don't forget the giant black cross hanging from my neck and ears. It was so much fun to copy Madonna, cuz no matter what, you looked so totally cool.

Other, favorites were the Flash dance over-the-shoulder sweatshirts, acid wash jeans, OP shorts, Izod and Ralph Lauren polo tees (collars up), leg warmers, stirrup leggings, plaid Bermuda shorts, bandanas tied around your head, neck, or ankle, argyle sweater vests, bolo ties, jelly bracelets, Members Only jackets, Mother Karen pullovers, rugby shirts, keyboard sleeve sweatshirts, clam diggers, "Frankie Says Relax" T-shirts, and Ray Ban sunglasses just to name a few.

Then there were the jeans. You had to have the coolest jeans. Of course, that's been true in every decade. Back then, if you didn't have a swan, bull, or horse embroidered across your butt, you so weren't a Valley Girl. Gloria Vanderbilt, Sergio Valente and Jordache were must-haves in the eighties, followed by Levi's 501s, Guess jeans, and don't forget your favorite pair of Bongos, Calvin Kleins, or Z Cavariccis. All these brands cost a pretty penny, but that's what your parents' credit cards were for, duh!

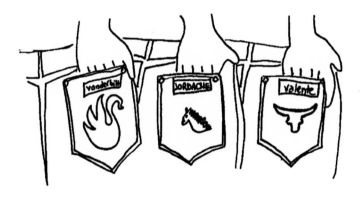

At forty, we do still love our jeans. Lucky brand seems to fit us right, as well as our long-time favorite, the Gap. We have ventured into the flare leg and low rise, but seriously, it's not a great look for some of us. Have you heard the phrase, "muffin top"? Well, it is no longer something you eat. The lower the rise on your jeans, the bigger the muffin. It is definitely one of the most bogus looking shapes ever seen. Hello? Are there any designers out there listening? Calvin Klein, it's no longer what's between me and my Calvin's. Its what's on top! HELP! Please bring our waistline up at least a couple of inches closer to the belly button. For heaven's sake, we look like breakfast walking around!

PARACHUTE PANTS

The scariest part of the parachute pants is that you can still buy them! There are several online stores that proudly sell them. They were rampant in the early eighties, with their nylon fabric, eight pockets, and ten zippers. Like, I'm so sure. Why did we need eight pockets and ten zippers that didn't unzip to anything? Then, an even scarier thing happened to them. By the late eighties, they decided to open the parachute and they added an eight to ten inch sag in the crotch. Thanks for that look, M.C. Hammer! Like, mega grody. I'm so sure, if you wore those today you'd have to take them off to get through airport security. You could smuggle a whole terrorist in that gap!

THE RASPBERRY BERET

Thanks to Prince we all had to have one. We did find various shades of raspberry, but in the end almost all Vals had and wore a raspberry beret in 1985, and I'm pretty sure most Vals didn't get theirs at a second-hand store. Gross!

Esprit

In 1968, Doug and Susie Tompkins started selling Esprit clothes out of their station wagon in San Francisco, CA; and by the eighties, Esprit sprung a logo wearing phenomenon. It became one of the most recognized and memorable logos in international fashion. I have to ask the question every Val wants to know. Where did it go? Does anyone know? I loved Esprit and had so many of their fun clothes, but I haven't seen an Esprit logo in, like, ten years. I guess Esprit is a thing of the past. Hey, if any of you Vals stumble upon the logo anywhere, give me a call so I know where I can get it. My number is 867-5309.

UNITS

What the heck? Do you remember this clothing line? Okay, so like your skirt today is your headband tomorrow and your jacket tomorrow is your shirt today? Somehow, it all worked. You just needed a few pieces to pull together the unit and then you could intermix them all you wanted. Needless to say, the idea didn't catch on past the eighties. It was way too confusing, especially for us Vals.

SHOES

One thing I love to reminisce and get a chuckle out of is the shoes we wore. The eighties really did have its own strange shoe fetish, but hey, we did have Imelda Marcos to keep up with. The shoes were sometimes strange and very uncomfortable, but that's beside the point. They were the style, and that is all that really mattered to us Vals. The must-haves were Jelly shoes (those things hurt), Espadrilles, Nike Sneakers, Penny Loafers, Flojos (loved my Flojos), Vans, Topsiders, Capezios, Converse high tops in any wild color (I had orange ones), L.A. Gear, Keds, Huaraches, and Peter Pan boots. (I hated those. We would tuck our jeans into them. Yuck!) Then came Dr. Martens—now those were cool. My grandmother thought I was kidding when I bought a pair of those.

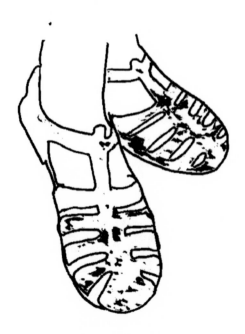

Then there were the feet that had to cram into all those shoes. As we now know, we needed to take better care of them. Cramming into pointy pumps in the eighties did its share of damage. We still love our designers, but have learned five hours in a pair of thirty-minute shoes is pure torture.

Body

Okay, so I'm totally thinking an alien, like, came in the middle of the night and did like an outer space body transfer on me. They, like, totally took my cute, tight, skinny body and left me this strange, mushy, saggy-skinned suit to cover my bones. The only problem is the suit doesn't fit. It's not the same size at all. It hangs funny in places, like my boobs and butt. The alien designer must have been a total bogus hack, because drawing lines that look road mappish all over is so not cute. Yeah, I'm pretty sure that's what happened to my body. I just woke up one day and it was gone.

Okay, let's get serious. The stereotype of a great body for a woman has changed just a bit from the eighties. I mean, our moms were no Demi Moores when they were forty. We have seriously unfair standards to keep up with today. I am a size twelve who forever seems to be dieting and exercising and still can't seem to lose five pounds. Unless I do some major crazy diet that eventually gets me down a size, but is impossible to stay on, to which I seriously fall off, and then wham, I'm a size fourteen and I'm worse off than when I started. I'm sorry, but *I'm hungry like the wolf,* and I can't do the no-carb, thousand-calorie-a-day stuff. I guess I just need to accept the fact. I am never going to be Gisele. But in my head, and to many other people who look at me, unless I can go below a size eight, I'm a huge, mega beastly cow.

It is so bogus! Yet, we Vals have long supported the culprit of all this unfairness: the clothing designers, magazine publishers, and movie producers who have decided the only beautiful women are the size nothings. Unfortunately, it has gone too far. There is probably no return for us Vals. It is stuck in our heads forever. Skin-covered skeletons have become our goal, and many of you have achieved it. As for the rest of us who actually have to eat, we can once again say thank God for the eighties. We ate our Doritos, drank our cherry Slurpees, and wore miniskirts at any size with no shame.

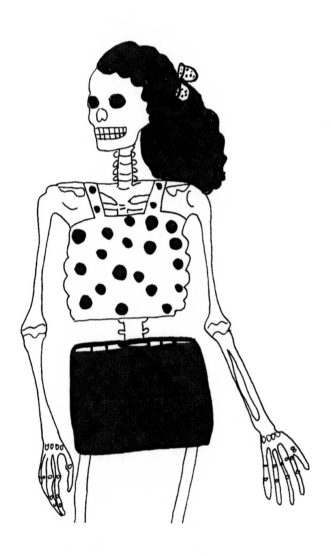

Totally Bitchen Eighties Stuff

Television

How cool was it. Reality TV was an unheard of idea, and we had this thing called characters and plots. In the eighties, TV families gave us a reason to tune in every week. I loved *Family Ties*, *The Cosby Show*, and *The Facts of Life*. Even more radical, I remember when all of America watched to find out who shot J. R. I mean, it was so much more fun than which whining, mascara-running bimbo the Bachelor is going to pick this season. Eighties TV is something I miss. Unfortunately, I think the idea is a thing of the past. So grab your fuzzy slippers, recline in your lazy boy throne, and take a look back at all our Val favorites!

The Cosby Show
Family Ties
Knott's Landing
Dallas
Dynasty
Miami Vice
Facts of Life
The A-Team

Knight Rider
Alf
Three's Company
Punky Brewster
Murphy Brown
Cheers
21 Jump Street
The Love Boat
Different Strokes
Growing Pains
The Greatest American Hero
Hart to Hart
Magnum P.I.
The Jefferson's
Hill Street Blues
Moonlighting
Night Court
Who's the Boss
Alice
Fantasy Island

Okay, so if you've been, like, living in a cave or something the last twenty years I will give the answer. Kristen, Sue Ellen's sister, shot J. R., because, duh, she was pregnant with his son. So she had to frame the always drunk Sue Ellen, because she was jealous of her, because she was married to him, of course. Like I'm so sure, why did you think she did it? Like duh, totally!

SMURFS

I loved the *Smurfs*. I watched that cartoon every Saturday morning. I loved Papa Smurf and Hefty Smurf and the blonde one, what was her name? Oh yeah, Smurfette. But my favorite was the narcissistic, attitude flying Vanity Smurf. He always had his little purple flower in his hat and was completely glued to his handheld mirror he carried with him. Gee, you think Ellen broke the gay barrier? I think the Smurfs did twenty years prior, ever so smurfly!

AMERICAN BANDSTAND

This was my favorite show of the week. I remember seeing and hearing Madonna for the first time on *American Bandstand*. I was in awe of her. She did "Holiday" and flitted around with dance moves I had never seen before. She was so bitchen. I also remember seeing Loverboy, Rick Springfield, Eddie Money, The Motels, Blondie, and so many others on *Bandstand*. It was a Val favorite. I guess American Idol resembles *Bandstand* a bit. Ryan is a close replica of Dick. The talent is there, but they aren't artists just yet. But hey, it sure is a fun show when it's eighties night.

THE WEDDING

We watched the Royals take the plunge two times in the eighties with Di and Charles and then Fergie and Andrew. We also turned out in record numbers when thirty million Americans tuned in to watch our favorite fake couple, General Hospital's Luke and Laura, take their vows. On November 16, 1981, we skipped school, work, and appointments to watch the highest-rated episode in soap opera history take place. Luke and Laura said "I do," and who could ever forget it? It was drama we wanted, and we sure got it. When Scotty showed up and caught Laura's bouquet and inevitably got pounded by Luke, it was so totally awesome!

OPRAH

What's up Oprah, you don't think you have any children? Well, duh, we are your children. Okay, maybe younger sisters, but still, we Vals have been with you a long time. We grew up over the latter half of our teen years with you, as fully dedicated viewers. I remember doing the shake diet after being astonished by your wagon full of fat. You have showed us more recently the correct way to shed those pounds, and you look fabulous might I add. We watched you when we were home with our babies, totally wigged out in the afternoon, and then it was four o'clock. Break time with Oprah. We are still watching you today as we enter our mid-life whatever it's called. Like, I seriously can't think of TV without you, Oprah. You are truly a bitchen lady. Thanks for all the info and fun over the last twenty-five years.

Movies

The things we saw and did when we were teens were just so impressionable. *I love eighties movies.* Hello, there was nothing better than *The Breakfast Club*, *Pretty in Pink,* and *St. Elmo's Fire.* I mean come on, these were totally rad movies. Of course, the most awesome movie ever made was … *Valley Girl.* Hello, Nick Cage was such a babe, and the music was the ultimate. The Plimsouls were so bitchen in it. The plot dealt with all our issues back then: falling in love, gnarly chick cliques, having to make a choice on your own. It was a tubular movie. I think HBO played it a million times, and I must have tuned in at least that many.

I have to say *Fast Times* was up there with *Valley Girl.* Who doesn't love Spicoli? He was such an awesome dude. Then there was *Sixteen Candles.* Jake Ryan was a totally buff babe. Of course, every girl longed for a best friend like Ducky in *Pretty in Pink.* He was a barney, but he was so sweet. See, there was just nothing like the movies of our generation. Here are some Valley Girl favorites:

Fast Times at Ridgemont High
Valley Girl
Sixteen Candles
St. Elmo's Fire
The Breakfast Club
Risky Business
Flashdance
Pretty in Pink
Footloose
Raiders of the Lost Ark
Tootsie
Crocodile Dundee
Fatal Attraction
Private Benjamin
Naked Gun
Turner and Hooch
The Karate Kid
Steel Magnolias
When Harry Met Sally
Nine to Five
Porky's
The Color Purple
Terms of Endearment
Ghostbusters
Weird Science
Mommy Dearest
Purple Rain
Back to the Future
Ferris Bueller's Day Off

And then there was this little alien creature who crashed landed on earth in 1982 and made us all want to get drunk on Coors beer, pig out on Reese's Pieces, and phone home—E.T. Who could ever forget this movie? It was a smash hit and broke all box office records for its time. Steven Spielberg, you are so mondo cool.

Valley Girl favorite movie quotes
The Breakfast Club (1985)

Brian Johnson: Dear Mr. Vernon, we accept the fact that we had to sacrifice a whole Saturday in detention for whatever it was we did wrong. But we think you're crazy to make us write an essay telling you who we think we are. You see us as you want to see us. In the simplest terms, in the most convenient definitions. But what we found out is that each one of us is a brain...

Andrew Clark: And an athlete...
Allison Reynolds: And a basket case...
Claire Standish: A princess...
John Bender: And a criminal...
Brian Johnson: Does that answer your question? Sincerely yours, the Breakfast Club.

(I mean, it's like Valley Girl Shakespeare.)

Valley Girl (1983)

Julie: Do you think she really does all the stuff she says?
Stacey: I mean, who could make up "that stuff tastes like Clorox"?

Julie: Yeah, but Tommy can be such a dork, ya know? Like he's got the bod, but his brains are bad news.
Suzi: But he is bitchen. You really are so lucky, Julie.
Julie: I know, but we've been together so long now. Like, I'm beginning to think I'm a piece of furniture or something … like an old chair!
Loryn: Oh, bad news!
Julie: (glancing at Brad) I definitely need something new.

Poltergeist (1982)
"They're heeeere."

(Oh my God, I didn't sleep for a week!)

Sixteen Candles (1984)

Samantha: Donger's here for five hours, and he's got somebody. I live here my whole life, and I'm like a disease.

Ginny: I really love Rudy. He is totally enamored of me. I mean, I've had other men love me before, but not for six months in a row.

Ghostbusters (1984)

"Listen you smell something?"

Ferris Bueller's Day off (1986)

"Life moves pretty fast. If you don't stop and look around once in awhile, you could miss it."

"Um, he's sick. My best friend's sister's boyfriend's brother's girlfriend heard from this kid who's going with a girl who saw Ferris pass out at 31 Flavors last night. I guess it's pretty serious."

Pretty in Pink (1986)

"Blaine? His name is Blaine? That's not a name that's an appliance."

"I remain the Duck Man."

St. Elmo's Fire (1985)

Alec: You're being arrested for drunk driving.
Billy: Drunk definitely, but I don't know if you could call it driving.

Wendy: No diet works. The only way to lose weight in the thighs is amputation.
(At forty, I'm thinking this might be true.)

Back to the Future (1985)

Marty: Why do you keep calling me Calvin?
Loraine: Well that's your name, Calvin Klein. It's written all over your underwear.

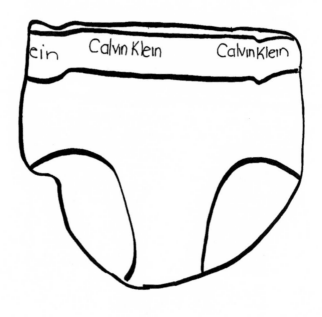

Fast Times at Ridgemont High (1982)

(Spicoli has a pizza delivered to class)

Mr. Hand: Am I hallucinating here, or just what the hell do you think you're doing?
Spicoli: Learning about Cuba and having some food.

Spicoli: What Jefferson was saying was, Hey! You know we left this England place 'cause it was bogus; so if we don't get some cool rules ourselves, pronto, we'll just be bogus too! Get it?

Brad Hamilton: Why don't you get a job Spicoli?
Spicoli: What for?
Brad Hamilton: You need money.
Spicoli: All I need are some tasty waves, a cool buzz, and I'm fine.

THE BELOVED BRAT PACK

In June 1985, a New York magazine article reported on the group of young actors taking Hollywood by storm. The Brat Pack it was tagged, and the Brat Pack it became. The cast of this famous group, who played roles in all the eighties coming-of-age films, were all Val favorites.

Robert Helper Lowe (born in 1964). Which makes him a mid lifer too. I love the Lowe. I actually met him at a Starbucks a couple years ago in Beverly Hills. He is such a Baldwin and he smells so good, ladies. Oh, and did I mention he can act! He is still making movies and is in a new totally awesome television show. Rob you are just so mondo cool to the max.

Alexandra Elizabeth Sheedy (born 1962). She is such a great actress. I was always so amazed at Ally. I mean, she "had" to work with all those hunks and sometimes "had" to kiss them, and she could still seriously act after that. I mean, c'mon, the average girl back then would have seriously needed to call all her girlfriends and write twenty pages in her diary before she could ever go back to work. That is if, she didn't faint first. Wow, Ally, you must have serious super powers.

Demetria Gene Guynes (in case you're an airhead, "Demi Moore," born in 1962). If Demi were my friend I would always call her Demetria. I could just never get past that opportunity to tease her. Geez, you'd have to grab the obvious. I mean, she's gorgeous, she's so talented, and she's married to Ashton. Hello, you have to seize the opportunities when they knock. I'm, like, so sure!

Judd Asher Nelson (born in 1959).Wow, I love his middle name, but yikes, he is almost fifty! He is so talented, and I have loved him in everything. He was always the dark, mysterious, bad boy we all wanted to date, but could never bring home to dad.

Michael Anthony Thomas Charles Hall (born in 1968). He is actually older than me, but I guess he will always seem "Farmer Ted" aged somehow. I loved him in every nerdy role he ever played. He is a great actor. He made us love all the total Melvins out there. In a sweet, brotherly way of course.

Andrew T. McCarthy (born in 1962). Huge crush on you, Andrew, huge. What does the "T" stand for? Totally Hot, I bet. Oh, Andrew, you were my favorite brat, and you obviously never got my telepathic messages I sent you in 1985. I would send them to you daily, letting you know I was available and ready to be your girl. It's a shame, Andrew, we would have been so good together.

Emilio Estevez (born in 1962). He has no middle name, at least none that I can find, so I gave him one. We can call him Emilio Two-Bit Estevez. Loved him in that role. Emilio, I can't imagine the eighties without you. You are one super fine dude who made us Vals swoon. You are so totally talented too. Oh, and did I mention super fine?

Molly Kathleen Ringwald (born in 1968). She was so totally awesome. I wanted to be Molly. I seriously wanted to dye my hair so I could look just like her. She is a super talented actress who was in almost every great eighties movie, and she got to make out with Andrew McCarthy in *Pretty in Pink*! Hello, she was the luckiest girl in the eighties.

There were others who almost made the pack but didn't. Maybe they weren't bratty enough. They certainly were talented enough: Tom Cruise, Matt Dillion, C. Thomas Howell, Ralph Macchio, Charlie Sheen, Kevin Bacon, Mary Stuart Masterson, Matthew Broderick, John and Joan Cusack, Patrick Swayze, Kiefer Sutherland, Robert Downey Jr., Sean Penn, and Jon Cryer, to name a few.

TOM CRUISE

Why does everyone hate Tom Cruise? I love Tom Cruise. He has brought us Vals much joy in the eighties with his movies. *All the Right Moves, Born on the 4th of July, Cocktail, The Color of Money, Legend, The Outsiders, Risky Business, Taps, Top Gun*—and those are just from the eighties. He has been making movies for over twenty-five years. Most of the girls I knew had at least one poster of the Cruise hanging on their wall in their bedrooms, and you know half of you would endlessly stare at it wondering how you could meet him and make him your boy. He was a huge crush. We Vals called it the "Cruise Crush." He was so darn cute it actually hurt to watch him.

So he fell in love and got a little excited about it on the Oprah show. So he showed his ignorant man side by dissing Brook Shields on a topic no man should have an opinion on. But seriously, how many men have said stupid things publicly? Okay, his Scientology stuff is weird too, but that's only because it's not my thing. I am saddened by all the airheads out there that bash the Cruise. He is a truly gifted actor who has entertained us for many years. I say if we have to put up with nauseating zods like Brittany and Paris, who constantly make the human race look tweaked, then our cutie the Cruise can love his wife and enjoy his religion until his heart's content. Like, I am so sure, whatever!

Music

Like, where does one even start with the music from the eighties? It was by far the most tubular and completely awesome era of music. There has never been and never will there be anything like it again. Here are just a few of our favorite bands.

The Go-Go's (#1 of course)
Duran Duran
Devo
INXS
Psychedelic Furs
Thompson Twins
Howard Jones
The B-52's
UB-40
Modern English
The Smiths
David Bowie
The Police
Stray Cats
Def Leppard
Bon Jovi

REO Speedwagon
Foreigner
Madonna
Human League
Pat Benatar
Katrina and the Waves
Chaka Khan
Men at Work
Eddie Money
Simple Minds
Prince
Talking Heads
Billy Idol
Berlin
Spandau Ballet
The Bangles
Bananarama
Oingo Boingo
Blondie
Night Ranger
REM
Tears for Fears
Bruce Springsteen
AC/DC
Huey Lewis and the News
Like, I am so sure I could
seriously go on forever.

Spandau Ballet

Every Val remembers "The Ballet" as we called it. The song that will forever ring in our hearts or in any elevator you might get in from here on out: "True" It was "Truly" the only song the band ever had. They did hit #4 on the U.S. Top ten with it, making them a Valley Girls favorite. But their time in the spot light was short lived, and by the end of 1984 they were gone, it was so true.

Van Halen

Okay, I had to say something about Van Halen. I mean, it's Van Halen! I finally got to see them in concert after twenty five years, and they rocked! However, I did observe something quite disturbing that evening. What's with all the eighties rockers who haven't stopped wearing spandex and never cut their hair? I mean, I must admit, it was entertaining for like a second, and then it just got creepy. Hello. David and Eddie cut their hair, and they weren't wearing spandex. Creepy to the max, fer sure.

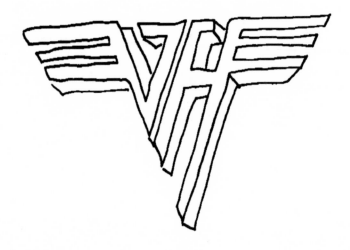

Boy George

George Alan O'Dowd. Some people would ask, "Is it a girl or a boy?" I never doubted. Hello, freak me out, if the George was a girl, super grisly girl. But we can all rest assured he was a boy. I am assuming he still is one as well. I must admit, I haven't followed up on him. He wasn't one of my favorites, but he sure sold records. He had six top-ten singles, and we can all remember getting our grove on to "Karma Chameleon" and of course "Do You Really Want to Hurt Me?" I don't remember the rest. Like I said, not my fave.

LOVERBOY

"Everybody's Working for the Weekend," "Only the Lucky Ones," "The Kid is Hot Tonight." Ahh, Loverboy, who could ever forget them and their music? Even better, who could ever forget the red leather pant–wearing butt of lead singer Mike Reno with his fingers crossed over it? Totally hot!

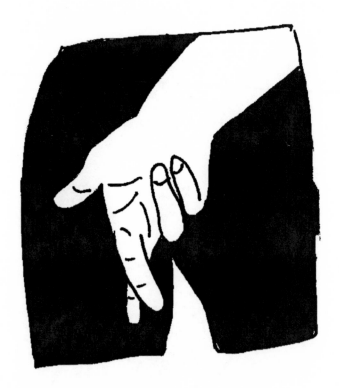

CYNDI LAUPER

Cynthia Ann Stephanie Lauper. I loved the Lauper. She was so unusual and so was her album. She was definitely a Val favorite. I loved how she could take a hot pink, orange, and green dress, add striped socks and a yellow and black polka-dot sweater, throw on a ton of makeup, rat up her very Frenchy pink hair, and look absolutely, totally cool. Like, no one else could ever do that. "Girls Just Want to Have Fun" is still one of my favorite songs and will remain in Valley Girls' hearts and ringtones for years to come.

MICHAEL JACKSON

In the eighties, the King of Pop was born. Well, his awesome music was born anyway. He swept us away with all his moves, grooves, and his eighties style. Michael Jackson is one of America's most beloved pop culture stars of all time. Like they did with the Beatles, girls would scream at the very presence of the Michael. His most notorious hit, which is still imitated in endless movies and YouTube videos, was "Thriller." Who could ever forget the dance, the zombies, and the song? We have loyally played it every Halloween for the last twenty-five years. The album *Thriller* has sold more than 46 million copies, making it the best-selling record of all time. That is something! Of course, let us all not forget that it was an eighties musician who set a record like that. Awe, eighties music, you just can't *beat it.* Personally, my favorite Michael time was his Jackson Five days. He was so cute and innocent back then. I loved "ABC" and "I'll Be There." Unless you've been a total space cadet over the last fifteen years, I don't have to explain to you the cloud of suspicion that has followed the Michael around. It is sad and hopefully not true, so I think I will keep my memories of him way back when he was on top of the music world and not on top of anything else. Yikes, total barf city.

VIDEO KILLED THE RADIO STAR

Literally at the stroke of midnight, on August 1, 1981, MTV launched. The first video was "Video Killed the Radio Star" by the Buggles. It changed the way we listened to music, because now we were actually watching music. It was so totally brilliant. All our favorite songs and bands came to life. We learned bitchen dance moves, like Michael Jackson's moon walk, and many stories were told through music videos. However, towards the end of the eighties, something happened. MTV actually killed the video stars. They turned the long loved station into a reality freak show. I thought the "M" in MTV stood for music. I guess that's now a thing of the past. I must admit I do enjoy an occasional hour of *Punked*, but that is really the exception. I miss it. I don't want TV. *I want my MTV.* Hello, MTV, you taught us that, as if!

THE GO-GO'S

The first time I heard the Go-Go's was in 1981. I was in the sixth grade. I really didn't care much about music back then. I thought people only sang songs about clouds in their coffee, and to be honest, for the longest time I thought she was saying clowns in my coffee! That totally freaked me out. Hello, I was only eleven.

But then one day I heard a different sound. It had a beat unlike anything I had ever heard before. This beat made something inside me move. My heart raced, my head spun, and the voice that sang along belonged to one of the coolest chicks my ears and eyes had ever encountered. "We Got the Beat," the Go-Go's, Belinda Carlisle … oh my gosh, I had arrived! The Go-Go's were it for me. I know the sixties chicks had their Beatles, but the Go-Go's were all eighties. Their look, style, music, and beat were all so totally brilliant. Out of all fads, phases, and fashion statements, my favorite look of all time was the Belinda. She was just so totally bitchen all the way around. Her hair, clothes, moves, and of course her voice just spoke total coolness always.

GO·GO'S

My chick clique and I have been fans from way back in junior high. We have played their music endlessly. The Go-Go's got us through many broken hearts, and nothing said let's celebrate our friendship more than blasting the Go-Go's every chance we got. Belinda, Gina, Charlotte, Kathy, and Jane, you Vals rock, and it has been so stellar to be your fan over the last twenty-five years. I only have one request left. Please tour one more time. I promised my thirteen-year-old daughter I'd take her to one of your concerts, and see, I can't do that if you don't come back.

Stuff

The eighties was the era when materialism birthed its ugly self onto a generation, and we have never gone back. We found instant gratification in buying stuff, and then more stuff. We certainly grew up with more than our parents had, and now our children have more than we could have ever imagined. I'm so sure, it's such a tweaked way to live. We buy, buy, buy, and then in, a year or so, when the style has changed or there is a new and improved version, we re-buy the same crap. It has become a totally bogus and insane trap. It started with Atari—your house was just not cool unless you had an Atari system. Then came the Sony Walkman. If you were a Val, you could not be seen in public without a Walkman attached to yourself. I mean, you totally had to have and use one all the time or people might think you were a total wanker or something. Duh!

Other must-have material girl things were:
Boom box
Cassette tapes
Combs with big handles
Honda scooters
Hacky sacks
Monchichi
Puffy stickers

Spuds MacKenzie key chains
Trapper Keepers
Swatch watch
Varnet sunglasses
Digital clock radio
Pee-Chee folders
Velcro
Wallet
Dophin shorts
Waterbed
Your own phone

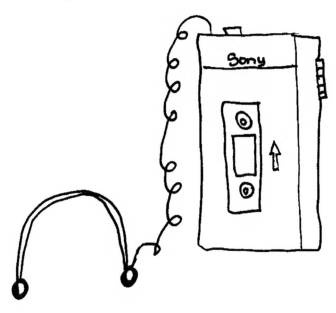

Cabbage Patch Kids

Okay, so I was ten in 1980, and the Cabbage Patch craze began in 1983, totally beyond my doll playing days. However, I do remember it well, with its doughy looking carved face and its little birth certificate. The madness of this doll! Every girl ten and under in America had to have it. This was one of the first but certainly not the last time that Americans lost all self-control. Getting a hold of one of these at Christmas in 1983 was a nightmare, and American parents were in a state of panic.

RUBIK'S CUBE

Ahhh! The thought of the cube still frustrates me. This zany cube was invented by a Hungarian professor of architecture named Erno Rubik. I often wondered if he spent his nights in the eighties laughing at us, as we lay in our beds for hours on end trying to get it. I never got it! This thing was bigger than my brain could twist. It was also bigger than life in the eighties. Over one hundred million cubes were sold. Can you believe it? Much to my dismay, it has found its way back. My kids now each own a Rubik's cube. One of these days, Mr. Rubik, I will figure it out and you will no longer be laughing at me!

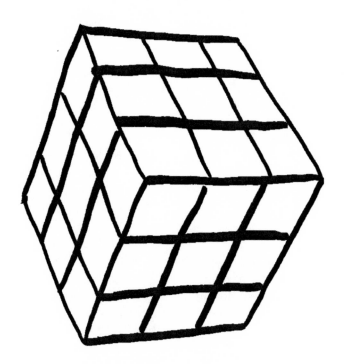

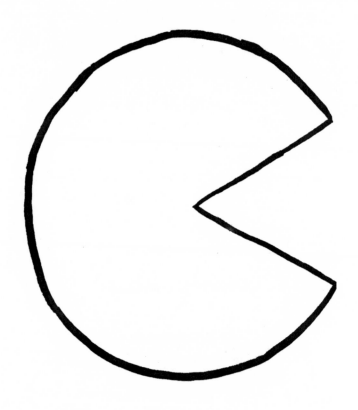

Pac Man

Remember our gobbling little friend that swooped the nation? He was our first video game star. Timeless hours were spent chomping dots and running from the little ghosts with big eyes. Wow, the memories I can still hear the sounds … Rer rer … Rrrrer rrrer rrrer.

You Can Take the Girl
out of High School, But
You Can't Take The High
School out of the Girl

High School.com

We had no idea back in the eighties that we would have this amazing thing called the Internet. Like I am so sure, wow, if we had only known how different our lives would be! This amazing tool, as you all know, can be very fun. Especially, if you love to keep up on old high school friends, flames, and fools, you are only a click away. There are numerous high school alumni sites where you can see where they are, what they are up to, and maybe even how they look. Like, some of them totally even post their pictures! However, with all the high school reminiscing, you must remain a smart Val. If you are going to log on and check out an old flame, be careful, because you can easily lose your head and send them an e-mail (that is a scary thought), because you don't want to look like you even care or ever think of him at all. Most importantly, you definitely want to make sure he hasn't turned into some psycho.

Like, sometimes, I think the memory of them is better how they were back then, and you might just be surprised how totally jerkish they have gotten. Have fun and send e-mails, but be careful. Usually, once a mega-dick, always a mega-dick!

High School Reunions

Reunion time is when all our good standards and morals get dropped, because we have to be someone other than ourselves to survive it. I wonder why we put ourselves through this torturous event? This will always remain a mystery to me. Why do I go? Why does anyone go? Seriously, I think it is a disease and we who go are seriously ill.

With that said, I guess there is a level of excitement in seeing how everyone is doing. Even more important, how everyone looks, and of course, most important, how do you look? I swear, when a reunion comes around, I can lose serious amounts of weight. After turning thirty, it is truly the only weight-loss program that works! Of course, there are reasons for all this weight loss and looking hot. THE BIG CRUSH. What if he is there? Worse, what if he is still a bitchen babe? You don't want to come rolling in looking like an oompa loompa! Grody to the max. Yep, that is a serious reason to get yourself hot.

Even more serious than the big crush is that most vicious, ragged out, mega bitch club that existed in everyone's high school memories. Imagine rolling in with your double chin and running into those chicks! Freak me out, fer sure. But imagine being super gorgeous and then running into them and they are the oompa loompas. Now, that is a seriously wicked thought. Like, I'm so sure, I know we shouldn't care so much, but come on, let's be real. We Vals have always cared, and we still do and always will. Like I said, it is a bogus disease we Vals have.

You   *Them*

The Guys

Well, by now most of them are men. Notice the word "most." Yes, it's true some of them aren't quite there yet, even at forty. It is interesting to think about how they might have all turned out. We Vals definitely categorized them into their different groups, and today I think those categories still fit most of our eighties dudes.

The jock. He could have gone either way. He could still be at home with mommy driving his '83 mustang around, daydreaming daily about the big game that never happened. Or he could have decided to put the football on the shelf next to his trophies and grow up. He could be a great dad and husband, coaching all his kid's sports teams and learned to love the game from the sidelines.

The nerd. Well I think we all know what happened to most nerds. They grew up and are most likely gorgeous hunks of men who have tons of success and money, because they started planning it all out twenty years ago. But the flipside of the nerd is if they didn't grow up like this, they very well could be the freaky weirdo guys who end up on *America's Most Wanted*! Super scary thought, but it could be true of some of the nerds you knew.

The surfer. Okay, hopefully this isn't true for most of our Spicolis out there, but the scariest thought is that his main form of transportation is still his skateboard. Yikes. Which means he is probably working at a cannabis club or something. Which speaks for itself as to where his life has gone. But maybe he put the bong down a long time ago and is, like, an awesome marine biologist or coffee shop owner. I think we can all agree the surfer is probably not sitting behind a desk all day.

The preppie. Again, he could have gone either way. He could still be wearing his Sperry topsiders with no socks, which inevitably means if he gets away with that at the office, he probably doesn't have a job that amounted to much. Or he could have folded his polo collar down, and is into the cola kind of coke now. He may have done well in college, and he is now a successful businessman and a great guy.

Girls' Night Out

Girlfriend time has totally changed for us Vals. We used to have big slumber parties and stay up all night pigging out on Doritos, red vines, and wine coolers (that we had to bogusly shoulder tap for). We would crank call every boy we had a crush on. Then we would go tee-pee the boy that lived the closest. After that we would call them again to see if they liked any of us and then we would spend the rest of the night just talking about all the boys, and what jerks they were if one of them said no. It was so totally awesome.

Well girls, the times have totally changed for us here. Good news is we are totally legal to drink now. Cosmos, margaritas, martinis—whatever your mood desires. The bad news is we're forty and, well, some of us have become quite boring! Girls' night out is always shortened or missed because of many totally bogus reasons. Here is just a few.

- **The husband**.
- Calls you to let you know he is an idiot and can't handle two hours of his own children.
- Wants his dinner.
- Has to work late
- Is a complete control freak and you're not even at girls' night out.

- **Children.**
- Way too busy with too many activities they can't keep up with—and neither can you.
- One of them is sick. An excusable one, but when overused we know you are full of sushi, totally!

THE WORST ONE.

You are forty, you came out, but it's 7:30 PM and you're tired after one drink, and you want to go home and be an old lady.

Girls, we have to stop! These are our friends. These are the people we will laugh with and reminisce with when we are parked in our wheelchairs at ninety. We have so many memories, but we have to keep making them. Even if we only have a few Girls' Nights Out a year, make them good ones!

Spin Cycle

Love

Love, ahhhh! It's in every song we have ever heard. It's all we ever wanted as Valley Girls growing up. But now, at forty, *what has love done for you lately?* By now, we have realized that love is not the crazy ongoing affair seen on daytime TV. I am happy not to be living under that lie anymore. It has taken many good and bad times, tears and jeers, to get us where we are today in our love lives. We have learned what is real and what is complete ignorant fantasy. By now, we are in one of three categories: married, divorced, or still single. In all three, we have learned so very much. None are easy, and none are that bad. It is what it is at this point in your life. You may be single after a bogus divorce or in absolute marital bliss. But whatever cards you were dealt, you are a Val, and you have made the best of it.

Married

Your wedding day, the happiest day of your life. Yes, but staying together for a lifetime, making love work with one person for the rest of your life, really is nothing short of a miracle. Somewhere along the marriage path, we hit bumps, loss of romance, loss of passion. I mean, it is the same person day in and day out, ladies. Same guy, same everything, but when you think about it, how great is that? Why do we always think we need so much change? Our lives are constantly changing around us. To me, this is my one sacred thing, my partner for life. I say maximum brilliant to you Vals lucky enough to have found it, worked it, and are living it. Marriage to one person for the rest of your life is a totally awesome thing.

Divorced

Wow, this is a hard one. It is hard to find the good in a divorce. Unless, well more than likely, it was something stupid he did. Then for sure you don't want him anymore anyway. I think somewhere along the way we forget that being married to someone means you made a lifetime commitment—it wasn't just a thing you agreed to because you wanted to have a big party. When you cross that altar, I think and hope you Vals are completely sure of the love and commitment you are about to make. At the same time, you are thinking that vow is being made to you. For better or for worse, till death do you part. That is why it is so gnarly.

I have watched many of my friends and clients go through divorce. It is such a wicked thing. There are many reasons a marriage doesn't work. They all aren't the same, and none of them are easy. You just can't find a lot of good in it. However, being a Valley Girl, I did manage to find a little humor. Did you hear about the new Barbie doll out this year? She is divorced, and she comes with all Ken's stuff! Okay, I know, totally shallow, but if you are one of the many women out there who was dumped for a younger girl, at least you have the "law of half" on your side. I know having stuff doesn't make the pain go away, but being a Val, we do like to have our stuff. So if he pulled something like that, then taking half of his stuff can be lots of fun, too. Of course, most importantly, remember you are a Val and don't give up on love. It will definitely find you again. You have learned more about marriage than anyone. You could probably write a book on what you have learned. You will find your new way, and he will be a total Baldwin.

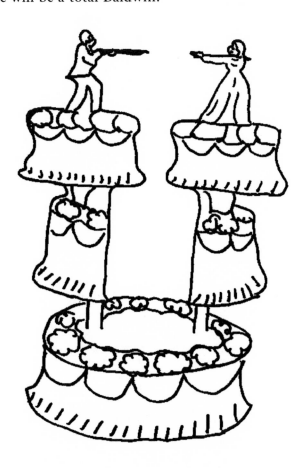

Single

Maybe you are totally where you want to be, forty and single. Good for you, but I have a hunch there are more of you that are longing to find "love" and be married, and you are pretty fed up with the fish in the sea you've been swimming in. It has been awhile for me in the dating game, but I remember it like it was yesterday. So you're going along great, the excitement level is so intense, you can't wait to see each other. When you do, there is so much passion, you wish you could bottle the feeling so you could have it always. I mean, it couldn't be any better at this point.

Then, no call for two days, then it's two weeks, and you start calling him because you think you must have done something. You start to apologize for a whole bunch of little over-analyzed nothings you've conjured up in your head. As painful as it is and as strange as it seems, one day it is absolutely perfect and the next day your whole life has changed. You just want to hit the rewind button and get out of this twilight zone you've suddenly found yourself in.

Put the brakes on, girls. Realize, you deserve to be someone's most precious total princess—you are a Val, for heaven's sake. Remember in the movie *Valley Girl* when Randy (Nick Cage) says to his friend, "That chick Julie, she's truly dazzling." If we have learned anything in our forty years, it is that we all deserve to be adored like that. I assure you, Randy never would have dissed Julie—ever! So pull yourself together, get back out there, and find your Randy! He will stop the world and *melt with you.*

Motherhood

So this is how I picture most of you Vals as you entered motherhood. So like, you totally got pregnant, couldn't wait to go shopping and find super cute maternity clothes, and found that as your belly and feet grew, they became less and less cute. Then, at the ripest you ever imagined your cute bikini-wearing belly could ever grow, boom, it's labor time. Of course, you totally got all the drugs you could talk your doctor into. You were so excited to meet your new bundle of joy and cherished the very second the doc handed her to you. In your life, you never imagined that you could be this happy without spending a zillion dollars and having it gift wrapped in a little blue box.

You bring that little bundle home and quickly find out there are no instructions on this little cutie. Wow, you never imagined it could be this tough, that something so cute and so sweet could be so insane and so scary all at once. You definitely didn't breast feed, cuz, eww, gag me with a nipple or something? You are so not the type to whip out the girls and give anyone a free show, let alone your designer bras can't smell like spoiled milk! Plus, you have free huge Dolly Parton sized boobs right now. You just want to keep them cute and dry, cuz hey, that's about all the sexy you have left at this point.

Now your sleepy, tired, swollen, stretched, and fat new body has to figure out how this little baby works. Crying, feeding, sleeping, pooping—oh, and did I mention crying? You slowly start to get the hang of it. Before you know it, she is now two, three, four, and she has found her voice and has many very important questions for you, like, "Mommy what is a Versace?" and "Why are we at the mall again?"

Then it's off to elementary school. Of course, she has the cutest clothes that match all her hair ribbons, socks, and backpacks. You find yourself super appalled at how some of the kids show up looking like they rolled right out of bed and for that matter rolled all the way to school. Didn't their moms ever have Barbie dolls? Then you meet their moms and you kind of figure it out.

Before you know it, they're off to junior high. At this point, you start to kind of remember things from the times when you were there, especially the mean girl stuff. Totally bogus and totally never changed. See, there are always going to be totally lame zods, and then those zods have children. I guess it's part of the circle of life or something. It totally sucks, but that is how it goes. So then it's high school. You find yourself pausing. "Wait, didn't I just get out of there? How can I be old enough to actually have a high schooler?" It doesn't stop there; we are only at mid-life, ladies. Let's hope none of you at forty are grandmas just yet. That is another book in itself, so I'll have to get back to you on that.

The Three Taboos

Religion

Wow, I am so blessed to have found my faith. I can't imagine getting through the milestones in my life without my Jesus. There is so much peace in knowing Him.

I don't understand why some are so freaked out by people of faith. Like, I am so sure, people today seem to think that worshipping and following God is weird. I guess many bogus people have done some pretty stupid things and made a lot of faiths look pretty gnarly. But people do a lot of stupid things all the time. Having faith in God gives you hope and security. I can't imagine wondering what would happen to me if I died without knowing the answer through my faith. I encourage you to shop around for a church. C'mon, you know you like to shop. Well, it is the same thing when it comes to church. It's like trying on a pair of jeans—you definitely have to find the one that fits you perfectly.

Politics

I think politics have become just as bogus as turning forty. What's with everyone? When did America become so divided? When did we become left vs. right? We used to be Democrats and Republicans, and we had a little of both in every one of us. Both parties should be ashamed. Politics have become an ugly, beastly freak show. If the candidates really got to know us (the people) again, they would find we really don't care about their opponent's bogus real estate deal twenty years ago, or whether they smoked pot at seventeen.

I mean, we have all had grisly stuff in our lives, and who really cares anyway? We need jobs that pay us enough to take care of our families and buy us an occasional pair of Jimmy Choos. We need to have health care and retirements, and for God's sake, we need to pay our teachers and schools enough so our children can have all the opportunities we had. They are the people who are going to take over our world when we are the oldies. If our politicians would stop bickering and stop spending zillions on attacking each other and just pay attention to us, the people again, maybe we could solve some of America's real problems.

Ah, who am I kidding? It's probably gone too far. People have forgotten what's important. I'm not even sure some of them know why they are voting for the person they vote in. It has become a bogus rumble of libs vs. cons, and I'm just embarrassed by all of us. We have become such spoiled, whining brats we've forgotten how to share our ideas respectfully. We have forgotten how to get along and forgive each other. It's like we have become unmanageable two-year-olds.

My fifteen-year-old son is probably the smartest person I know. His teachers and youth group leaders constantly praise him not only for his excellent grades and manners but for his character and heart. Many have encouraged him to run for President one day. When I ask him, "What do you think, Matt? You are smart enough, patriotic enough, your character is that of a leader, so how about it?" His reply is, "No way! It would be hard enough to have all the pressure of running this country on your shoulders, but to have half the people you are laying your life down for, end up hating you and all the people who voted for you because they don't agree with every single thing you do? Not for me. I am not that big of a sucker, Mom." Wow, remember the day when the dream of being president was a totally righteous goal? At this point, I vote for Ferris Bueller for President.

War

Another cherished item from our youth was the vet. Okay, so I'm not talking about a Corvette. The vet I am talking about is the Vietnam vet. You may be asking, "What does this have to do with a Valley Girl turning forty," but if you think about it, they were totally part of us Vals' hearts. They were our dads, uncles, and brothers. Over time, I have often wondered what today would look like if the sixty thousand American soldiers who lost their lives in Vietnam were alive. What would the eighties have looked like? I totally think they would have become some of the most awesome men America had ever known—doctors, scientists, teachers, movie stars, designers. Who knows, maybe one of them would have found the cure to cancer or the magic pill that could make you lose twenty pounds overnight. It's an interesting thought to imagine what our world would look like had they all lived. I guess their purpose was what it was—an incredibly honorable purpose, the pursuit of liberty and justice for those in need. What's really amazing is they didn't choose their own path. Most of them were given it. They bravely gave their lives fighting in a war they might not have believed in, but I assure you they believed in the country and government who sent them there. For that—for the bravery, courage, and patriotism of these soldiers—I say thank you. I am amazed at the lives you lived, and I will until the day I die salute you from the bottom of my argyle sweater–covered heart.

I Want to Go Back!

Recently, I went to an Eddie Money concert. He is just timeless really. I mean, yeah, he has gotten a bit older, as did the rest of us, but he is still one tubular rocker after all these years. Anyway, like I was saying. I went to the concert and he sang "I Want to Go Back." (C'mon, you remember the song: "I want to go back and do it all over, but I can't go back, I know.") That song sums it all up for me. I loved the eighties. I loved everything the eighties had to offer: the music, the movies, the clothes, the hair, the stuff, and of course, most importantly, my youth.

So I'm turning forty. How bad can it really be? I mean, yeah, like the song says, I wish I could go back, but I'm pretty sure the Delorean is forever locked up at Universal Studios. So unless Richard Branson decides to invent a "Virgin" time machine, I guess I'll just have to get used to the 2000s. Is that what we call this era?

It's not going to be easy. I think the Valley Girl is in my DNA. I love big hair, big clothes, and big shopping sprees. At forty, I have found myself with nothing but a big mortgage, big tax bills, and a big, busy schedule that doesn't include a shopping mall in it anywhere.

Oh well, I guess I should just accept my age, enjoy my accomplishments, and settle down into this thing called mid-life. I mean, turning forty means you have lived forty years, and that is pretty amazing in itself. Living life is a totally cool thing.

I should be thankful for the last forty years, thankful Ronald Reagan didn't push the big red button, thankful I didn't marry my prom date, and thankful I never ended up on the cover of National Enquirer. See? It's already totally looking up. As if.

Printed in the United States
207033BV00001B/223-228/P

9 780595 529339